Myunghwa Jang

Interpretation of Beethoven's Fidelio or Leonore and four different overtures

GRIN Publishing

Bibliographic information published by the German National Library:

The German National Library lists this publication in the National Bibliography; detailed bibliographic data are available on the Internet at http://dnb.dnb.de .

Imprint:

Copyright © 2010 GRIN Verlag, Open Publishing GmbH
Print and binding: Books on Demand GmbH, Norderstedt Germany
ISBN: 978-3-640-77360-2

This book at GRIN:

http://www.grin.com/en/e-book/159536/interpretation-of-beethoven-s-fidelio-or-leonore-and-four-different-overtures

GRIN - Your knowledge has value

Since its foundation in 1998, GRIN has specialized in publishing academic texts by students, college teachers and other academics as e-book and printed book. The website www.grin.com is an ideal platform for presenting term papers, final papers, scientific essays, dissertations and specialist books.

Visit us on the internet:

http://www.grin.com/

http://www.facebook.com/grincom

http://www.twitter.com/grin_com

Interpretation of Beethoven only one opera *Fidelio* or *Leonore* and four different overtures.

1. Background

By the early nineteenth century Ludwig Van Beethoven (1170-1827) had been widely regarded as a prolific composer of instrumental music. Recognizing that he was going deaf, Beethoven fell in and out of periods of great depression. It was also a time in which Viennese "fairy opera" and sentimental singspiel had become the popular music genre.

In 1803 Beethoven was commissioned by a director, Emanuel Schikaneder (1751-1812) to compose an opera for his theatre, *Theatre an der Wien*. Emanuel Schikaneder was mostly famous for his collaboration as a librettist with Mozart on popular operas such as *Die Zauberflöte* (The Magic Flute).[1] After abanding his first project *Vestas Feuer* (Vesta's Fire). Beethoven began composing *Leonore*, later entitled *Fidelio* in order to distinguish it from earlier pieces of the same name by other composers like Pierre Gaveaux (1761-1825) in 1789, Ferdinando Paër (1771-1839) in 1804, and Simon Mayr (1763-1845) in 1805.[2]

Finding himself living in the same city where Mozart died in poverty some 15 years earlier, Beethoven was intrigued by the

---

[1] Douglas Johnson, "Fidelio," in *The New Grove Dictionary of Opera*, 2 vols., ed. Stanley Sadie (London: Macmillan Press, 1992):183.

[2] Ibid,:186.

1

strength of the human spirit and the idea of good triumphing over evil.

Beethoven had always been drawn to the ideals of the opera genre

known as "rescue opera."[3] A "rescue opera" is an opera in which the

hero, after suffering many dangerous obstacles, including death,

ultimately prevails. A great admirer of opera composer, Luigi

Cherubini, Beethoven wanted to compose in a similar style.[4] For

example, Cherubini's *Les deux journées* (Lyric Comedy in three acts

1800, a libretto by Jean-Nicola Bouilly) is a "humanity" opera with a

subject that appealed to him, whereby he unreservedly admired

Cherubini's cool, precise, and fastidious music.[5] Beethoven chose to

compose an opera based on an adaptation of Jean-Nicolas Bouilly's

(1763-1842), French Libretto, leonore, ou L'amour conjugal (On

Conjugal Love), classic rescue story.[6]

Written with librettist Joseph von Sonnleithner, Beethoven's first

version was divided into three acts in the style of a German *Singspiel*:

spoken dialogue alternation with songs, and sometimes ensembles,

choruses, or more extended musical pieces. *Fidelio* was first

performed on November 20, 1805 after being delayed due to

censoring issues.[7] The opera opened to a small audience and negative

---

[3] Carl Dahlhaus, *Ludwig van Beethoven: Approaches to his Music*, trans. Mary Whittall (Oxford: Clarendon Press, 1991): 181.

[4] Johnson, op. cit.: 183

[5] James Parsons, "Fidelio," in *International Dictionary of Opera*, 1 vol., ed. C. Steven Larue (London:St. James Press, 1993):436.

[6] Michael C. Tusa, "Beethoven's essay in opera," in *The Cambridge Companion to Beethoven*, ed. Glenn Stanly (New York: Cambridge University Press, 2000):200.

2

reviews. This was not entirely Beethoven's fault. At the time of the opening, Vienna was occupied by French troops. Because of this, many of Beethoven's friends and usual patrons had fled the city. Therefore, his audience consisted of French nobility who found the opera to be less than spectacular. The few friends in attendance that evening were less than pleased with the opera as well, claiming the performance was too long. To Beethoven's disappointment, the show was closed after only three performances.[8]

A year later, Beethoven attempted a revision of *Fidelio* for the same theatre. Due to a change in management, Beethoven was presented with a new librettist by the name of Stephan Von Breuning.[9] After a great deal of struggle, a very reluctant Beethoven agreed to a much more condensed and concise version of the opera. The newly revised version was performed on May 29, 1806. Again the audience was not Beethoven's ideal audience and the show failed once again. Beethoven, a bit bitter, blamed the theatre management and quickly withdrew his opera proclaiming, "I do not write for the galleries."[10] It would be many years before Beethoven would try another hand at revising *Fidelio*. After the 1806 production, Beethoven quickly produced a great number of highly acclaimed

---

[7] Douglas Johnson, "Fidelio," in *The New Grove Dictionary of Opera*, 2 vols., ed. Stanley Sadie (London: Macmillan Press, 1992): 183.

[8] Tusa, op. cit.: 200.

[9]Ibid.: 200-201.

[10] James Parsons, "Fidelio," in *International Dictionary of Opera*, 1 vol., ed. C. Steven Larue (London: St. James Press, 1993):437.

3

works including the Symphony No.3, Op.55 *"Eroica"* and his Fifth

Symphony, Op.67.[11] However, he could not escape "his baby,"

Fidelio.

Years after its second attempt and failure, three singers wished to
revive Beethoven's Fidelio for Vienna's Karntnertortheater forcing
Beethoven to evaluate his opera one last time. After reading a refined
libretto by Georg Friedrich Treitschke, Beethoven agreed to the
revival but insisted on a complete revision in which he virtually
started over.[12]Nearly every number was altered in some fashion. The
third and final version of the opera opened with great success on May
23, 1814.

There has also been a great deal of discussion regarding
Beethoven's influences while writing *Fidelio.*[13]There is no doubt he
was influenced by Mozart's *Die Zauberflöte* (The Magic Flute),
utilizing similar concepts of dark versus light, good versus evil. It is
also interesting to note that it was *Die Zauberflöte*'s librettist,
Emmanuel Schikaneder who commissioned Beethoven's original
version of *Fidelio.*[14] Though it is not known whether Beethoven had
seen earlier settings of the story, there are clear similarities. Douglas
Johnson writes of the similarities in key structure and musical gesture

---

[11] Bary Cooper, *Beethoven* (New York: Oxford University Press, 2000): 140.

[12] Thomas K. Scherman and Louis Biancolli, *The Beethoven Companion* (Doubleday& Company, Inc., 1972):655.

[13] Michael C. Tusa, "Beethoven's essay in opera," in *The Cambridge Companion to Beethoven*, ed. Glenn Stanley (New York: Cambridge University Press, 2000): 208.

[14] Ibid.: 208.

4

as they relate to the different characters.[15] Those Characteristics are found in both Gaveaux's and Paer's versions. Like many composers, he pulled from own body of work as well, borrowing from his abandoned opera *Vesta Feuer* among other works.[16]

a: *Vestas Feuer*

b: O namenlose Freude! Duett Act II, Scene 5 from *Fidelio* in 1914

---

[15] Douglas Johnson, "Fidelio," in *The New Grove Dictionary of Opera*, 2 vols., ed. Stanley Sadie (London: Macmillan Press, 1992) :186.

[16] Ibid.: 186.

2. The Overtures to Fidelio

It took Beethoven over a decade to complete his only opera. Throughout the many revisions, he produced four different overtures. The first, now known as *Leonore* No. 2 was written for the opera's premiere in 1805. Because some sections proved to be too difficult, Beethoven began reworking the overture for the opera's revival in 1806.[17] The new version became known as *Leonore* No.3 Beethoven's final revision composed for the 1814 production was called the *Fidelio Overture*. After his death a fourth overture was found entitled *Leonore* No. 1. It is believed that he either wrote it first or for a production of *Fidelio* in Prague that never happened. *Leonore* No.3 is often played between the two scenes in Act two. Felix Mendelssohn introduced the practice, common until the middle of the twentieth century, of performing *Leonore* No.3 between the two scenes of the second act, and some conductors still perform it there. However, many critics, such as Henry W. Simon, consider this practice to be "abhorrently inartistic" due to the dramatic nature of the piece.[18]

Leonore Overture No.2 in C major played at the first performance of *Leonore*. This principal numbers is an Adagio, C major, 3/4 introduction, in which Florestan's aria "*In des Lebens Frühlingstagen* (In the Spring Days of Youth)" from the second act appears; an

---

[17] Ibid.:183.

[18] Henry W. Simon, *100 Great Operas and Their Stories* (New York: Doubleday, 1989) : 177.

Allegro C major, 2/2 containing the principal themes of the *Leonore* No.3 with the two trumpet calls (a little louder, taken directly from the opera). Gradually *crescendo* brings a climax with same subject fortissimo in the full orchestration. The second theme appears in E major in the cellos, and *arpeggio* figure sounding above it in the first violins. The development section, which is based on the material of the principal theme, carries in at the closed a unison passage in all the strings which lead into a chord of E flat; an *Adagio* in C major episode reproducing the Florestan aria which eventually gives way to a new theme developed in the violins leading up to a stirring, vigorous Coda and Finale.[19] It is stated by some authorities that the overture was withdrawn because the wind instrument parts were found to be too difficult.[20] Others are of opinion that after the first performance of the opera Beethoven was dissatisfied because the overture did not clearly express his ideas.[21]

Leonore Overture No.3 is a majestic overture. It opens with an *Adagio* in C major, 3/4 *fortissimo*, in full orchestra, followed by a scale passage which some critics conjecture describes the descent into the gloomy depths of Florestan's dungeon.[22] Following this passage, the clarinet and bassoon sing Florestan's dungeon aria, "*In the spring days of Youth*," with string accompaniment. Immediately mysterious

---

[19] John N. Burk, *The Life and Works of Beethoven* (New York: Random House, 1946): 319.

[20] Ibid.: 319.

[21] Ibid.: 319.

[22] Henry W. Simon, 100 Great Operas and Their Stories (New York: Doubleday, 1989): 180.

preludings are heard in the strings, it is accompanied by lighter work in the flutes, first violins and bits from the Florestan theme given out by the basses. A short climax is followed by an outburst of the full orchestra leading to the *Allegro* in C major, 2/2. It opens *pianissimo* with the first theme announced by the first violins and cellos in octaves against a sustained *tremolo* in the violas, and timid rhythmic pulsations in the double basses; a *crescendo* in the initial figure of the theme with full orchestra. Its development leads to a *fortissimo* in which the theme is elaborated at considerable length. The second theme is introduced in the horns, then passing to the first violins and flute against agitated triplet *arpeggios* in the second violins and violas; it begins in E major, then passes by a beautiful and sudden modulation to F major, then through G minor, A minor, and B major back to E major. As the development draws to a close a climax is reached, after which ensues a dramatic episode of great power, in which the trumpet calls each time announce the approaching deliverance, followed by a fervid and impressive song of thanksgiving.[23] The third section of the overture opens piano in G major, with a flute solo. A crescendo follows, after which the theme is repeated *fortissimo* and developed most elaborately. The second theme now reappears in C major, followed by development from the first theme, leading to the Coda which his *presto* and starts with rushing scale passages in the first violins, which are soon together by

---

[23] Thomas K. Scherman and Louis Biancolli, *The Beethoven Companion* (Doubleday & Company, Inc., 1972): 605.

the second violins, then by the violas, and, at last, by the basses, leading to a *fortissimo* outburst of the all orchestra on the first theme and closing the overture with an overwhelming outburst of gladness and triumph.[24]

Leonore Overture No. 1 Opus. 138 was laid aside and was not played in public during the composer's lifetime. The score and parts, in a copyist's hand, but with corrections by Beethoven, were discovered after the composer's death.[25] When it was recognized as an overture to the opera was not unnaturally arrived at. It resembles the *Fidelio* Overture in E major, Opus.72. The overture begins with a somber chord and a long, slow introduction. An impressive *crescendo* drives and accelerates without ceasing, towards the principal theme. Florestan's theme enters in the guise of a development, following the reprise of *allegro*.

Fidelio Overture was played for the first time at the Kartnerthor theatre in Vienna on May 23, 1814.[26] The overture opens with a short unison *Allegro* in the string and wind instruments followed by an *Adagio* in the horns and clarinet. The opening measures are then repeated and the *Adagio* reappears, the horn theme being taken in the wind instruments. After development the theme returns in the woodwinds, and again appears for the horn, leading to the main

---

[24] Ibid.: 606.

[25] Henry W. Simon, *100 Great Operas and Their Stories* (New York: Doubleday, 1989): 177.

[26] Michael C. Tusa, "Beethoven's essay in opera," in *The Cambridge Companion to Beethoven*, ed. Glenn Stanley (New York: Cambridge University Press, 2000): 201.

Allegro of the overture. The wind instruments sound a *crescendo*

chord and the first theme is outlined by the second horn, answered by

clarinet, and then developed by full orchestra. The strings give out the

second theme which is briefly treated. In the closing section of the

overture the first theme is heard in the horns, accompanied by violin

passages. At the conclusion of the *Allegro* development the *Adagio*

episode returns, leading to the *Presto Coda* in which a familiar phrase

from the first theme is worked up to a climax of exultation closing an

overture which has been called "an example of perfect beauty."[27]

3. Analysis of Fidelio Op.72

•Don Fernando, Minister (Baritone)
•Don Pizarro, Governor of a state prison (Baritone)
•Don Florestan, a prisoner (Tenor)
•Leonore, Florestan's wife disguised as the boy Fidelio (Soprano)
•Rocco, jailer (Bass)
•Marzelline, Rocco's daughter (Soprano)
•Jaquino, doorman (Tenor)
•First prisoner (Tenor)
•Second prisoner (Bass)
•Chorus of watchmen, prisoners, and townsfolk[28]

The opera unfolds the story of Florestan is a noble Spaniard,

imprisoned by his evil enmity of Pizarro, governor of a gloomy

mediaeval fortress, used as a place of confinement for political

prisoners.[29] Pizarro was enabled secretly to seize Florestan and cast

him into the darkest dungeon of the fortress, at the same time

spreading a report of his death. Hearing this news, Florestan's lovely

---

[27] John n. Burk, *The Life and Works of Beethoven* (New York: Random House, 1946): 320.

[28] Douglas Johnson, "Fidelio," in *The New Grove Dictionary of Opera*, 2 vols., ed . Stanely Sadie (London: Macmillan Press, 1992): 183.

[29] Thomas K. Scherman and Louis Biancolli, *The Beethoven Companion* (Doubleday & Company, Inc., 1972): 656.

wife Leonore disguised as a man, Fidelio, obtains employment as
assistant to Rocco, the chief jailer of the prison. Fidelio has been at
work and has become a great favourite with Rocco as well as with
Marzelline, the jailer's daughter who is disposed to cast off Jaquino,
the turnkey, upon whose suit she had smiled till her love for Fidelio
came between. Rocco looks with auspicious eye upon the prospect of
having such an industrious and thrifty son-in-law as Fidelio promises
to be a comfort to his old age. The action now begins in the courtyard
of the prison, where, before the jailer's lodge, Marzelline is
performing her household duties. Jaquino who has been watching for
an opportunity to speak to her alone, resolves to ask her to marry him.

The duet, Jaquino and Marzelline, opens *Allegro* in A major which
is in A-B-A form. The duet, Jetzt, Schatzche, is like a Mozartian vein
which is based on a four note orchestral figure also, both the vocal
part and accompaniment are short breathed and *staccato*.[30] This duet
was the second number in the 1805 version of the opera; however,
Beethoven switched number from two to one in the 1814 version of
the opera.[31] The duet expresses simple thoughts in simple language.
After duet, Jaquino's proposing is interrupted by a knocking at the
door, and when he goes to open the wicket, Marzelline express no
sympathy for his sufferings, but proclaims her love for Fidelio as the

---

[30] Paul Robinson, *Ludwig van Beethoven Fidelio* (Cambridge University Press, 1996): 8.

[31] Michael C.Tusa, "Beethoven's essay in opera,"in *The Cambridge Companion to Beethoven*, ed. Glenn Stanley (New York: Cambridge University Press, 2000): 205.

11

reason why she must needs say no.[32] And this she does with an impatient reiteration of "No!" in which the bassoon supports her. Marzelline sings her longing for Fidelio and pictures the domestic happiness which shall follow her unison with him.

Mazelline's aria, *wär ich schon*, opens *with Andante Con moto* in C minor and later C major. This aria was originally the first number in the 1814 version of the opera which is like a *singspiel* style.[33] This aria is very light, airy, and cheerful which move from minor to major, as well as a faster tempo and with fuller orchestration.

After Marzelline's aria, Marzelline, Leonore, Rocco, and Jaquino sing *Mir ist so wunderbar*. This Quartet, *Andante sostenuto* in G major, is a canon which the four personages have the same expression like Marzelline delightfully who thinks of Fidelio's love; Leonore sees every danger in the dotingness, Rocco expects the couple's happiness, while Jaquino rigorously complains of the betrayal. This quartet is divided with sustained harmonies in violas and cellos to which clarinets and then flutes are later added.

After Quartet, Rocco sings an aria, *Allegro moderato*, 2/4 and later change to *Allegro*, 6/8 in B flat major, *Hat man nicht auch Gold beineben*. It is about praise of money, and, for young people who need to marry, Beethoven cut the aria in the 1806 version of *Leonore*. The two strophe aria is in a well established buffo tradition in which

---

[32] Henry W. Simon, *100 Great Operas and Their Stories* (New York: Doubleday, 1989) 178.

[33] Douglas Johnson, "Fidelio," in *The New Grove Dictionary of Opera*, 2 vols., ed. Stanley Sadie (London:Macmillan Press, 1992) : 185.

12

alternating sections in different tempo and meter correspond to the contrasting moods of the singer's encomium.[34] In the latter violins mimic the gold's "ringing and rolling".[35]

In the trio, *Allegro ma non troppo* later change to *Allegro molto* in F major, *Gut, Söhnchen, gut* is served as the final to act I in the 1805 version of *Leonore*. It is powerful motive development, energetic accompaniment especially in the strings and flying vocal lines. The music changes between like canon, imitative passages for the separate voices, and concerted moments where the three unite to sing the almost same words in harmony.[36]

After the trio, surprisingly a march, *vivace* in B^b major, begin with a mild mood. The 1805 version of opera *Leonore* did not have a march, instead of it playing an introduction.[37] While the two preceding notes which timpani, *pizzicato* lower strings and contrabassoon, Beethoven begins the tune on the third beat of the bar: it sounds like an upbeat and a downbeat, but truly occur on the first two beats of the measure like. It ends with almost suddenly like comic style.

After a march piece, Pizarro sings with chorus *Ha! Welch ein Augenblich!*, *Allegro agitato* in D minor, this aria is provided

[34] Barry Cooper, *Beethoven* (New York: Oxford University Press, 2000): 151

[35] Paul Robinson, *Ludwig van Beethoven Fidelio* (Cambridge University Press, 1996): 10.

[36] Robinson, *op. cit.*: 11.

[37] Michael C.Tusa, "Beethoven's essay in opera," in *The Cambridge Companion to Beethoven*, ed. Glenn Stanley (New York: Cambridge University Press, 2000): 205.

breathless pace with the essential elements. The orchestra played most of the work with inauspicious timpani, strings, syncopated *sforzandi* and near unrelieved brassy *forte*. This aria is one of the heaviest and most difficult for bass voice, also the vocal phrases are irregular and obsessed with the original tone of D natural.

After Pizarro's aria, the duet, Pizarro and Rocco, sing *Jetzt, Alter, Allegro con brio* in A major, represents Pizarro's seduction of Rocco and distinguished by full striking effects.[38] The orchestra accompanies Rocco's description of the victim with chords.

After duet, Leonore sings recitative Abscheulicher!, Adagio, and aria *Komm, Hoffunug, Allegro con brio* in E major. "The music frequently changes key, meter and tempo also closely follows her shifting emotions, above all her metamorphosis from anger to tranquillity. The *Allegro* that follows is introduced by a blazing fanfare on the horns whose energetic commentary accompanies her new found determination to the end."[39]

After Leonore's aria, first act finale comes in B^b major, starting with prisoner's chorus *O welche Lust*, after this originally in 1805 version of Leonore had Rocco's recitative *Entfernt euch jetzt! Nun, konnit ihr eilen?*[40] ; however, Beethoven cut it out in the 1814 version

---

[38] Robinson, *op. cit.*: 10.

[39] Paul Robinson, *Ludwig van Beethoven Fidelio* (Cambridge University Press, 1996): 13.

[40] Douglas Johnson, "Fidelio," in *The New Grove Dictionary of Opera*, 2 vols., ed. Stanley Sadie (London: Macmillan Press, 1992):185.

of *Fidelio*, after chorus sing Leonore and Rocco sing recitative *Nun Sprecht, wie ging's ?* and then sing *Noch heute!, Wir müssen gleich zu Werke schreiten* after this Marzelline, Rocco, Leonore and Pizaro sing *Ach, Vater, eilt!.*[41] After this piece Rocco and Pizarro sing Habt ihr wohl in Acht genommen and the five soloists and chorus sing *Leb wohl, du warmes Sonnenlicht.* "Beethoven has the musical courage and dramatic integrity to end his act rescessively in keeping with the anxious uncertainty of the situation."[42]

The second act begins with the introduction, Florestan's recitative *Gott! Welch Dunkel hier!*, and aria *In des lebens Frühlingstagen, Grave, Adagio, pocco Allegro* in F minor, A^b major and F major. Beethoven also composed in the 1814 version of *Fidelio* a new final section *Und spur ich nicht linde.* It is a musical delineation of Florestan's surroundings and mental anguish. "The orchestral introduction is piercing wind chords, moaning lower strings, ominous timpani, and syncopated runs and wandering harmonies, relieved only by a flicker of light after a D^b major cadence in the middle."[43]

After Florestan sings, melodrama, duet Leonore and Rocco sing, *Andante con moto* in A minor, *Nur hurtig fort.* Borrowing the technique of melodrama in which declamation is set against orchestral commentary from contemporary French Opera. Sustained trombone

---

[41] Ibid.: 185.

[42] Robinson, *op.cit.*: 16.

[43] Ibid.: 16.

tones spread a portentous atmosphere and a contra bassoon adds

weight and solemnity to the motif which describes the labor of

digging.[44] After the duet, Florestan, Rocco, and Leonore sing the

Moderato in A major, *Euch werde Lohn*, which is primarily about a

celebration of humanity. In the middle section played staccato and in

the coda section, the tempo increases a little bit.

After that Quartet, Pizarro, Florestan, Leonore, and Rocco, sing

Allegro in D major, *Er sterbe!*. It surrounds the essential action of the

drama. Next, in the duet Leonore and Floreatan sing, *Allegro vivace*

in G major, *O namenlose Freude!*. This song has given musical

expression to the love that has driven its action. In the middle section

the orchestral texture is thin and a gentle, in which violins anticipate

the opening arpeggios that prepare the recapitulation.

Finally, the end of opera scene was largely rewritten compared to

Leonore 1805 and 1806 versions.[45] "A long fanfare like crescendo, its

orchestration growing thicker as it rocks back and forth between tonic

and dominant, introduces a festive C major chorus of prisoners and

people."[46] The next section of the final set in A major *O Gott! Welch*

ein Augenblich! Is the musical and emotional opera; the tempo slows,

sostenuto assai, and the key shifts magically to F major. A long

---

[44] Paul Robinson, *Ludwig van Beethoven Fidelio* (Cambridge University Press, 1996): 17.

[45] Michael C. Tusa, "Beethoven's essay in opera," in *The Cambridge Companion to Beethoven*, ed. Glenn Stanley (New York: Cambridge University Press, 2000):205.

[46] Robinson, *op. cit.*: 10.

arching phrase, which makes its way repeatedly through the orchestra, is eventually embraced by the voices.

The closing chorus with ensemble, *Wer ein holdes Weib errungen*, in C major is based on a line from Schiller's *Ode to Joy*.[47] The opera ends with the triumph of Leonore through the entrance of the Prince, or the heroic element of the opera, and justice is restored. "The finale makes its ecstatic way to closure as fragments of the tune in the chorus alternate rapidly with more lyrical interventions by the quintet of soloists."[48]

4. Conclusion

Critics have cited Beethoven's music for being too emotional for rather two-dimensional stories. No one denies the music is incredibly emotional and dramatic. However, some speculate that though the music is beautiful, it does not match the lack of deep characters. Henry W. Johnson noted in his book, *100 Great Operas*, "Beethoven lacked Mozart's tolerance for human frailty and ambivalence," and that he "formulated the choices in his own life in similarly unambiguous terms."[49]

Today, Beethoven's *Fidelio* is regarded as one of the greatest operas in the repertoire, yet, unfortunately, it is rarely performed.

---

[47] Tomas K. Scherman and Louis Biancolli, *The Beethoven Companion* (Doubleday & Company, Inc., 1972): 659.

[48] Robinson, *op. cit.*: 17.

[49] Henry W. Simon, *100 Great Operas and Their Stories* (New York: Doubleday, 1989): 176.

Prior to his death Beethoven spoke with his friend and bibliographer, Anton Schindler. Of *Fidelio*, he said, "Of all my children this is the one that cost me the worst birth-pangs and brought me the most sorrow; and for that reason it is the one most dear to me."[50]

---

[50] Douglas Johnson, "Fidelio, "in *The New Grove Dictionary of Opera*, 2 vols., ed. Stanley Sadie (London: Macmillan Press, 1992) : 186.

Bibliography

Bokina, John. *Opera and Politics: From Monteverdi to Henze.* New Haven & London: Yale
    University Press, 1997.

Cooper, Barry. *Beethoven.* New York: Oxford University Press, 2000.

Dahlhaus, Carl. *Ludwig van Beethoven: Approaches to his Music,* trans. Mary Whittall.
    Oxford: Clarendon Press, 1991.

Johnson, Douglas. "Fidelio," In *The New Grove Dictionary of Opera,* 2 vols., ed. Stanley
    Sadie, London: Macmillan Press, 1992.

Kerman, Joseph and Alan Tyson. "Beethoven," In *The New Grove Dictionary of Music and
Musicians,* 3 vols., 2nd ed., ed. Stanley Sadie, London: Macmillan Publishers Limited, 2001.

Parsons, James. "Fidelio," In *International Dictionary of Opera,* 1 vol.ed. C.Steven Larue,
    London: St. James Press, 1993.

Robinson, Paul. *Ludwig van Beethoven Fidelio.* New York: Cambridge University Press,
    1996.

Scherman, Thomas and Louis Biancolli. *The Beethoven Companion.* New York: Doubleday
    and Company, Inc., 1972.

Simon, W. Henry. *100 Great Operas and Their Stories.* New York: Doubleday, 1989.

Tusa, C.Michael. "Beethoven's essay in opera: historical, text-critical, and interpretative
    issues in Fidelio," In *The Cambridge Companion to Beethoven,* ed. Glenn Stanley,
    New York: Cambridge University Press, 2000.

Score

Beethoven, Ludwig van. *Fidelio* (Full score). New York: Dover Publications, Inc., 1984.

Beethoven, Ludwig van. *Vestas Feuer* (Vocal Score). New York: G. Schirmer, Inc., 1983.

Unger, Max, ed. Beethoven: *Leonore No.1 Overture*. London : Ernst Eulenburg, Ltd., 1935.

_____. Beethoven: *Leonore No.2 Overture*. London : Ernst Eulenburg, Ltd., 1935.

_____. Beethoven: *Leonore No.3 Overture*. London : Ernst Eulenburg, Ltd., 1935.